Have You Ever Seen a Stork Build a Log Cabin?

Written by Etta Kaner · Illustrated by Jeff Szuc

Kids Can Press

For Yael, with love — E.K.
To the teachers at OCAD who imparted their wisdom
and taught me how to paint — J.S.

Acknowledgments
Thank you to Ed Rajotte for his explanation of hornets' nests, to Karen Li for
her edifying editing and to Jeff Szuc for his illuminating illustrations.

Kids Can Press acknowledges the financial support of the Government of
Ontario, through the Ontario Media Development Corporation's Ontario Book
Initiative; the Ontario Arts Council; the Canada Council for the Arts; and the
Government of Canada, through the BPIDP, for our publishing activity.

Published in Canada by
Kids Can Press Ltd.
29 Birch Avenue
Toronto, ON M4V 1E2

Published in the U.S. by
Kids Can Press Ltd.
2250 Military Road
Tonawanda, NY 14150

www.kidscanpress.com

The artwork in this book was rendered in acrylic.
The text is set in Bodoni.

Edited by Karen Li and Samantha Swenson
Designed by Marie Bartholomew
Printed and bound in China

This book is smyth sewn casebound.
CM 10 0 9 8 7 6 5 4 3 2 1

Library and Archives Canada Cataloguing in Publication
Kaner, Etta
  Have you ever seen a stork build a log cabin?/ Etta Kaner ; Jeff Szuc, illustrator.
(Have you ever seen)

ISBN 978-1-55453-336-7 (bound)
1. Animals — Habitations — Juvenile literature. I. Szuc, Jeff II. Title.
III. Series : Kaner, Etta. Have you ever seen.

QL756.K36 2010   j591.56'4   C2009-903622-3

Kids Can Press is a *Corus*™ Entertainment company

Contents

Have you ever seen a stork build a log cabin? 4

Have you ever seen a hornet build a paper house? 8

Have you ever seen a mouse build a grass house? 12

Have you ever seen a crawfish build a mud hut? 16

Have you ever seen a polar bear build an igloo? 20

Have you ever seen a fish build a stone house? 24

Have you ever seen a termite build a high-rise? 28

Play around the World! 32

Have you ever seen
a stork build a log cabin?

That's silly.

5

People build log cabins.
How could a stork build
a log cabin?

6

Storks also use wood to build their homes. The male brings branches, sticks and twigs to the nest. The female fits them in place. Stork nests can grow to the size of a small car.

Have you ever seen
a hornet build a paper house?

That's silly.

9

People build houses
with paper.

How could a hornet
build a paper house?

10

Female hornets make paper to build their nests. With their strong jaws, they scrape off bits of dead wood. The hornets chew the wood to turn it into a mush called pulp. They shape the pulp into a nest. When the pulp dries, it becomes paper — just like the paper in this book!

11

Have you ever seen
a mouse build a grass house?

That's silly.

13

People build grass houses.

How could a mouse build a grass house?

Harvest mice build their nests near the tops of tall grasses. The females use their teeth to shred grass leaves into narrow strips. Then they weave the strips into a round nest the size of a tennis ball. The leaves are still attached to the stem, so the nest changes color with the seasons.

Have you ever seen
a crawfish build a mud hut?

16

That's silly.

17

People build mud huts.

How could a crawfish
build a mud hut?

18

Red swamp crawfish build with mud, too. They dig
up mud with their mouths and legs to make a burrow.
They carry the mud in little balls to the entrance of
the burrow. There, they stack the balls to make
a chimney. Some chimneys can be as tall as
60 cm (2 ft.).

Have you ever seen
a polar bear build an igloo?

That's silly.

People build igloos.

How could a polar bear
build an igloo?

22

Female polar bears build dens in hard-packed snow. The female digs a tunnel with her paws. At the end of the tunnel, she scoops out a large oval room. Then she scrapes a small hole in the roof to let out stale air. The snow walls keep the den warm and cozy for the bear and her new cubs.

Have you ever seen
a fish build a stone house?

That's silly.

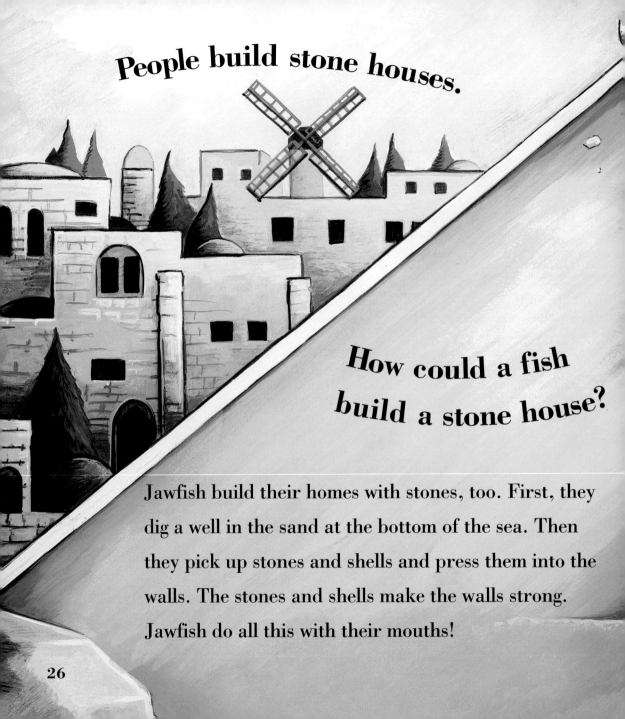

People build stone houses.

How could a fish build a stone house?

Jawfish build their homes with stones, too. First, they dig a well in the sand at the bottom of the sea. Then they pick up stones and shells and press them into the walls. The stones and shells make the walls strong. Jawfish do all this with their mouths!

26

Have you ever seen a termite build a high-rise?

That's silly.

People build high-rises.

How could a termite build a high-rise?

Some termites build tall mounds that are almost as hard as concrete. The termites use mud that has been chewed with grass. This makes the outside walls strong. Some mounds even have roofs to keep them dry when it rains!

Play around the World!

What is your home like? Is it the same or different than the homes in this book? Here's a chance to find out and win the game at the same time!

You will need

- 2 markers
- a coin
- a pencil
- the game board inside the cover, or make a photocopy

1. The first player flips the coin. Heads, he moves his marker one space; tails, he moves two.

2. He must say one way in which his own home is the same as and one way in which his home is different than the home where his marker is.

3. The next player follows the same rules.

4. The first player to reach the end wins. Good luck!

Need some help with ideas? Think about

- color
- shape
- size
- parts (roof, walls, doors, etc.)
- materials (wood, brick, mud, etc.)